Counting at the Zoo

Learning to Add 1 to One-Digit Numbers

Laurie Chilek

New York

I see 1 bear at the zoo.
Then I see 1 more bear.

That makes 2 bears!

I see 2 lions at the zoo.

Then I see 1 more lion.

That makes 3 lions!

I see 3 monkeys at the zoo.

Then I see 1 more monkey.

4 monkeys

That makes 4 monkeys!

Words to Know

bear   lion   monkey